Pebble®
Bilingüe/ Plus
Bilingual

Dientes sanos/Healthy Teeth

Vamos al dentista!
At the Dentist

por/by Mari Schuh

Traduccíon/Translation:
Dr. Martín Luis Guzmán Ferrer

Editor Consultor/Consulting Editor:
Dra. Gail Saunders-Smith

Consultor/Consultant:
Lori Gagliardi CDA, RDA, RDH, EdD

CAPSTONE PRESS
a capstone imprint

Pebble Plus is published by Capstone Press,
151 Good Counsel Drive, P.O. Box 669, Mankato, Minnesota 56002.
www.capstonepress.com

092009
005618CGS10

Books published by Capstone Press are manufactured with paper
containing at least 10 percent post-consumer waste.

Library of Congress Cataloging-in-Publication Data
Schuh, Mari C., 1975–
    [At the dentist. Spanish & English]
    Vamos al dentista = At the dentist / por Mari Schuh.
    p. cm. — (Pebble Plus bilingüe. Dientes sanos = Pebble Plus bilingual. Healthy teeth)
    Summary: "Simple text, photographs, and diagrams present information about going to the dentist and
how to take care of teeth properly — in both English and Spanish" — Provided by publisher.
    Includes index.
    ISBN 978-1-4296-4596-6 (lib. bdg.)
    1. Dentistry — Juvenile literature. 2. Teeth — Care and hygiene — Juvenile literature. 3. Children —
Preparation for dental care — Juvenile literature. I. Title. II. Title: At the dentist.
RK63.S3618 2010
617.6′01 — dc22   2009040919

Editorial Credits
Sarah L. Schuette, editor; Katy Kudela, bilingual editor; Adalin Torres-Zayas, Spanish copy editor;
    Veronica Bianchini, designer; Eric Manske and Danielle Ceminsky, production specialists

Photo Credits
Capstone Press/Karon Dubke, all

The author dedicates this book to her childhood dentist, Dr. Fred Carlson of Fairmont, Minnesota.

Note to Parents and Teachers

The Dientes sanos/Healthy Teeth set supports national science standards related to
personal health. This book describes and illustrates going to the dentist in both English
and Spanish. The images support early readers in understanding the text. The repetition
of words and phrases helps early readers learn new words. This book also introduces
early readers to subject-specific vocabulary words, which are defined in the Glossary
section. Early readers may need assistance to read some words and to use the Table of
Contents, Glossary, Internet Sites, and Index sections of the book.

Table of Contents

Tabla de contenidos

Teeth Checkups

Lena visits the dentist's office twice a year. Her teeth need a checkup.

Examen de los dientes

Lena va al consultorio del dentista dos veces al año. Es necesario que le examinen sus dientes.

Dentist Doug greets Lena.
He shows her where
to sit for her exam.

Doug, el dentista, saluda
a Lena. Le enseña donde
sentarse para examinarla.

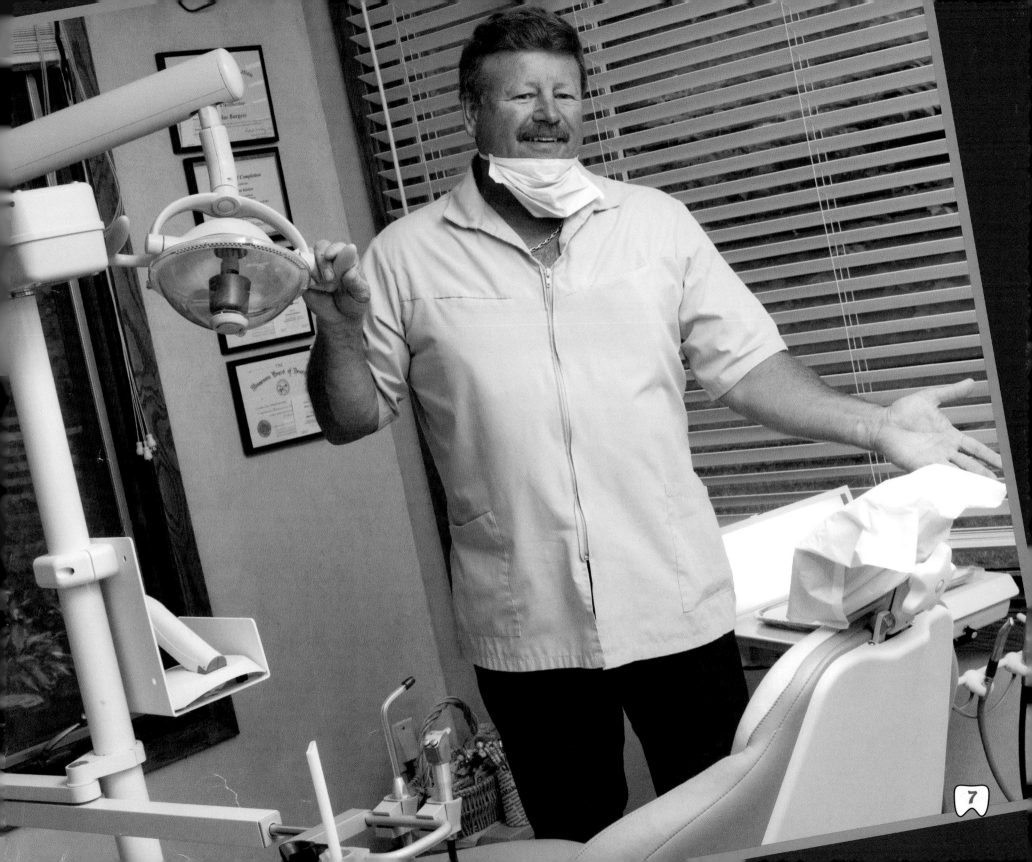

What Happens

Deb the hygienist teaches Lena about her teeth. Lena learns how to brush and floss.

Qué sucede

Deb, la higienista, le enseña a Lena lo que tiene que saber sobre sus dientes. Lena aprende cómo cepillarse y a usar el hilo dental.

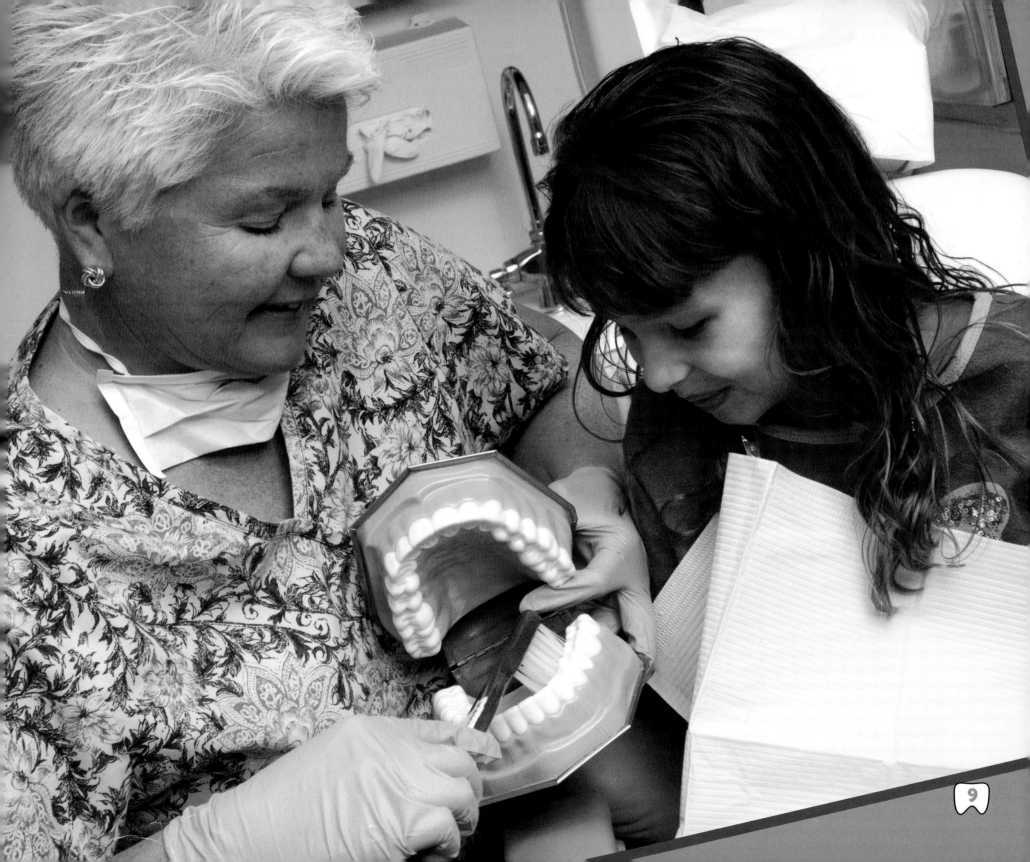

Lena has x-rays taken.

X-rays are pictures

of her teeth and gums.

Le toman unas radiografías a Lena.

Las radiografías son fotografías de

sus dientes y encías.

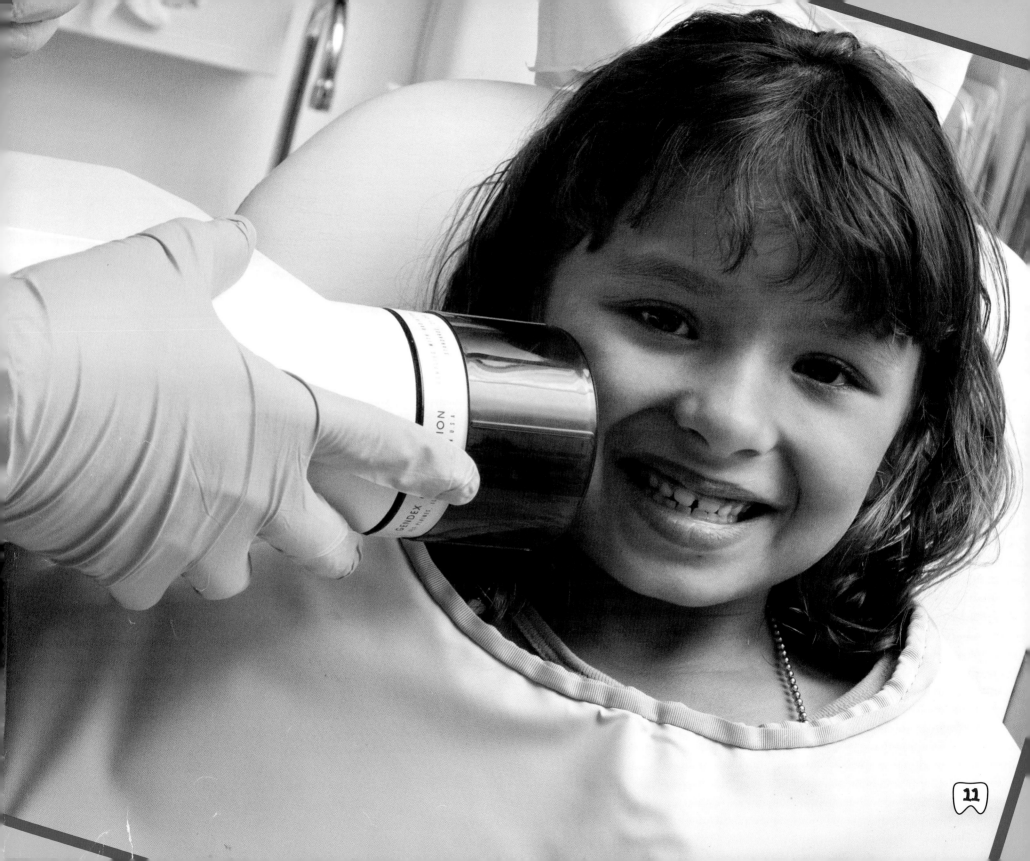

Deb cleans the plaque from Lena's teeth. Deb polishes and flosses Lena's teeth too.

Deb quita la placa que tienen los dientes de Lena. Deb también pule y limpia con el hilo dental los dientes de Lena.

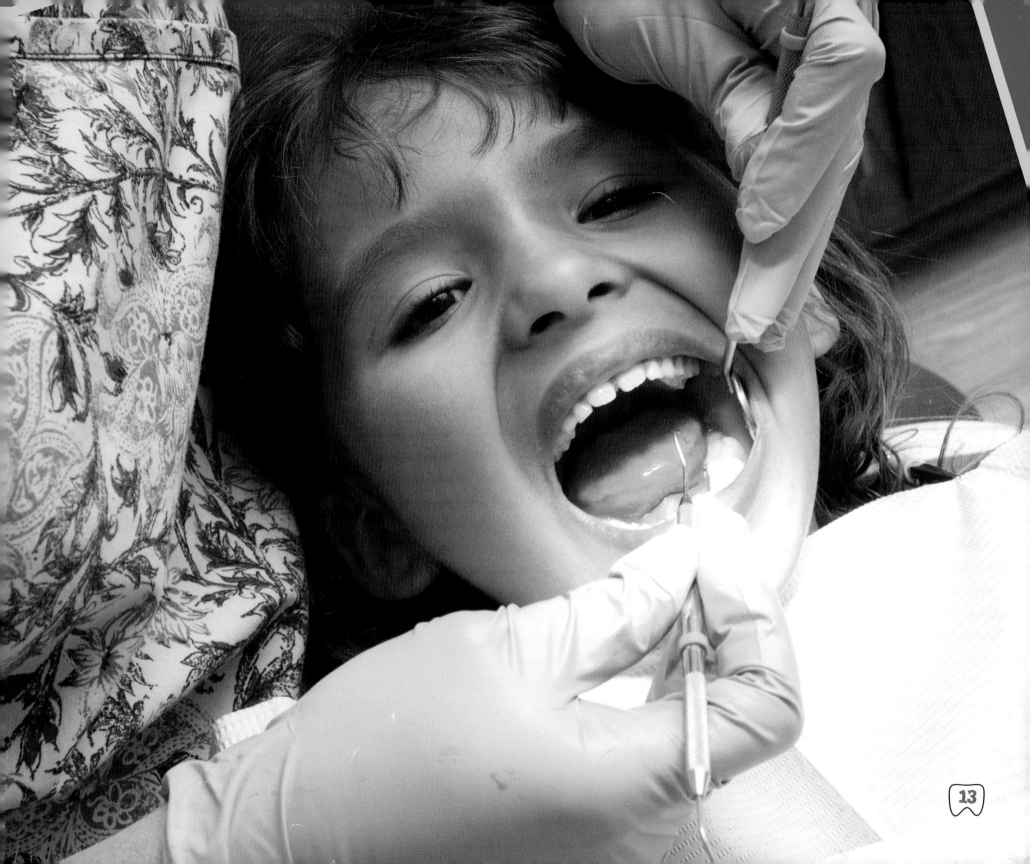

Cavities

Then Deb puts sealants on Lena's teeth. Sealants protect teeth from cavities.

Las caries

Enseguida, Deb le pone sellador a los dientes de Lena. El sellador protege a los dientes de Lena de las caries.

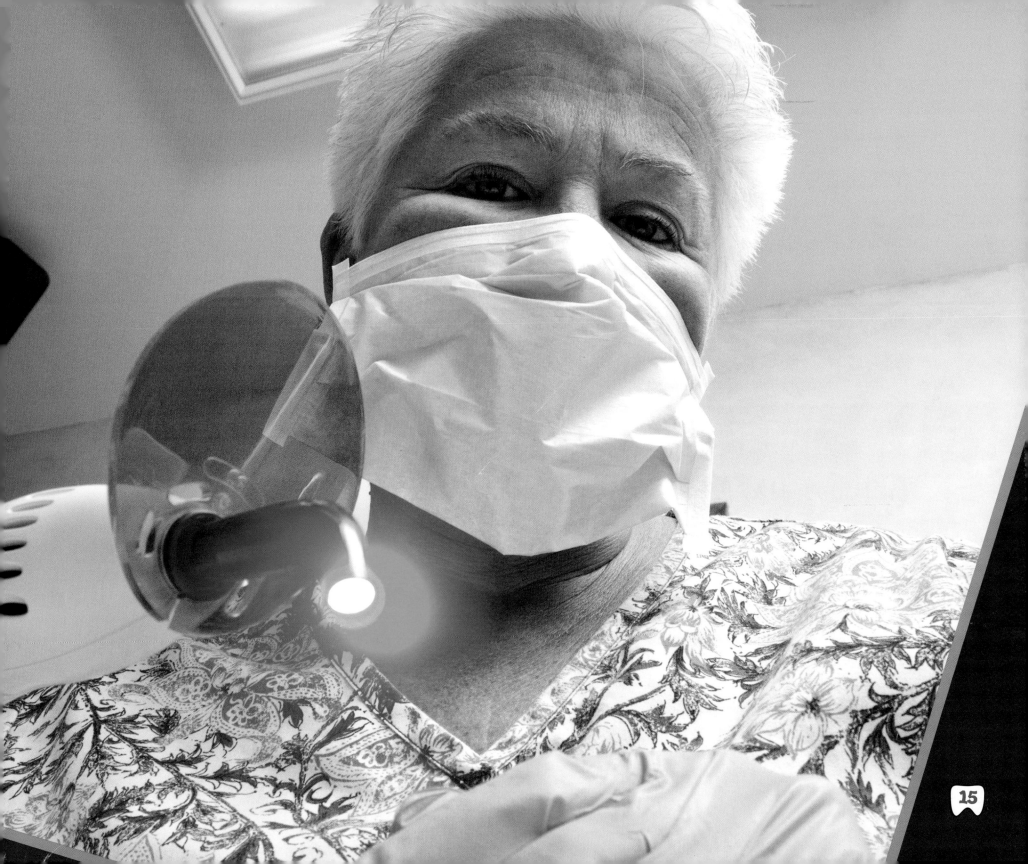

Next, Doug looks inside Lena's clean mouth with a small mirror. He checks for cavities.

Después, Doug revisa el interior limpio de la boca de Lena con un espejo pequeño. Examina que no tenga caries.

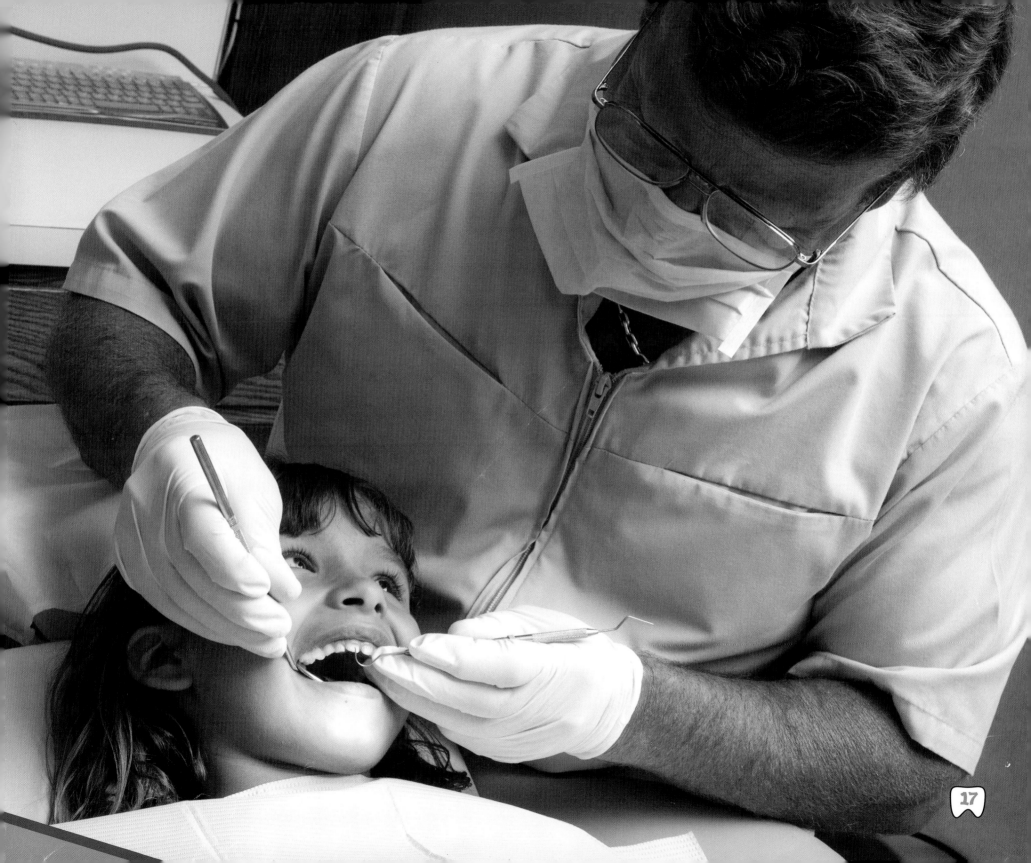

If Lena had a cavity, Doug would fill it. But Lena doesn't have any cavities. She's all done.

Si Lena tuviera una carie, Doug la taparía. Pero Lena no tiene caries. Ya está lista.

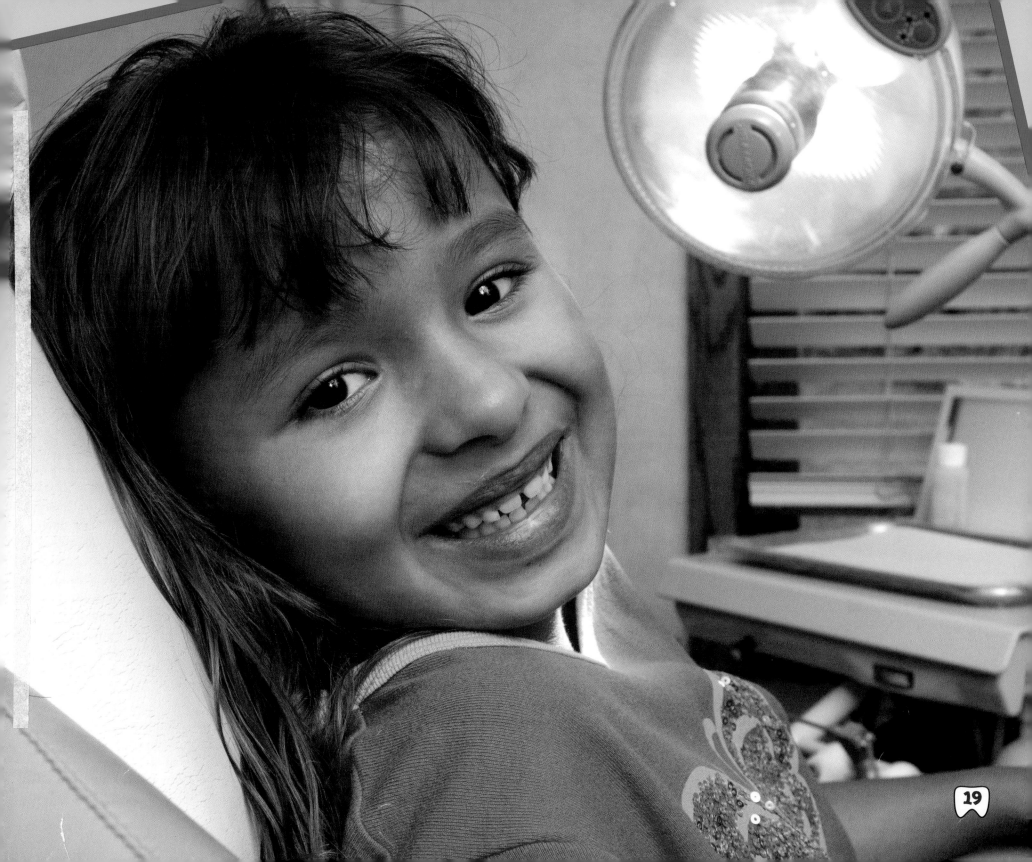

Healthy Teeth

Between dental visits, Lena brushes
and flosses every day. She will have
a clean, healthy smile.

Dientes sanos

Entre cada visita al dentista, Lena
se cepilla y usa el hilo dental todos
los días. Así tendrá una sonrisa
limpia y sana.

Glossary

cavity — a decayed part or hole in a tooth

floss — to pull a thin piece of dental floss between your teeth to help keep your teeth clean

hygienist — a person who is trained to clean, polish, and floss teeth; hygienists also take x-rays of teeth and apply flouride and sealants.

plaque — a sticky coating that forms on your teeth from food, bacteria, and saliva in your mouth; plaque causes tooth decay.

polish — to rub something to make it shine

sealant — a plastic coating put on your teeth to help prevent cavities

Internet Sites

FactHound offers a safe, fun way to find Internet sites related to this book. All of the sites on FactHound have been researched by our staff.

Here's all you do:

Visit *www.facthound.com*

FactHound will fetch the best sites for you!

Glosario

la carie — parte carcomida o agujero en el diente

el higienista — persona entrenada para limpiar, pulir y usar el hilo dental; los higienistas también toman radiografías y ponen fluoruro y sellador.

limpiarse los dientes con hilo dental — uso de un pedazo de hilo delgado que se introduce entre los dientes para mantenerlos limpios

la placa — capa pegajosa que se forma en tus dientes con la comida, bacterias y saliva que hay en tu boca; la placa produce deterioro en los dientes.

pulir — frotar una cosa para hacerla brillar

el sellador dental — una capa de plástico para cubrir los dientes que ayuda a prevenir las caries

Sitios de Internet

FactHound brinda una forma segura y divertida de encontrar sitios de Internet relacionados con este libro. Todos los sitios en FactHound han sido investigados por nuestro personal.

Esto es todo lo que tú necesitas hacer:

Visita *www.facthound.com*

¡FactHound buscará los mejores sitios para ti!

Index

índice